mummy
& me
cook

DK

LONDON, NEW YORK, MUNICH, MELBOURNE, and DELHI

Senior designer Gemma Fletcher
Senior editor Carrie Love
Designer Elaine Hewson
Photographer Dave King
Home economist Denise Smart
Production editor Raymond Williams
Production controller Ché Creasey
Jacket designer Rosie Levine
Managing editor Penny Smith
Managing art editor Marianne Markham
Creative director Jane Bull
Category publisher Mary Ling

First published in Great Britain in 2014 by
Dorling Kindersley Limited
80 Strand, London WC2R 0RL

Copyright © 2014 Dorling Kindersley

A Penguin Random House Company

10 9 8 7 6 5 4 3 2 1
001-196499-02/14

A CIP catalogue record for this book
is available from the British Library.

ISBN: 978-1-40933-847-5

Printed and bound in China
by Hung Hing

Discover more at
www.dk.com

Contents

Health and safety

In this book you will discover the basics about popular ingredients such as eggs and chocolate. You'll find out where they come from and how to cook them. Always be careful in the kitchen and follow the instructions.

Safety

All the projects in this book are to be made under adult supervision. When you see the warning triangle take extra care as hot cookers, electric appliances, and sharp implements are used to make a recipe. Ask an adult to help you.

Getting started

1 Read the instructions all the way through before you start.
2 Gather together everything you need so it's in one place.
3 Have a cloth handy to mop up any spillages.
4 Put an apron on and tie back your hair.

Key to symbols

prep time

cooking time

yield (serves or makes)

Food wise

• When you're in the kitchen you should ask an adult to take things in and out of the oven, and to use the hob.
• Wash your hands before and after you work with food. Always wash your hands after handling raw eggs and raw meat.
• Do not lick your fingers after you've worked with food.
• Check the use-by date on all ingredients.
• The dessert-type recipes are meant as special treats as part of a balanced diet.
• Carefully weigh out the ingredients before you start a recipe or project. Use measuring spoons, weighing scales, and a measuring jug as necessary.
• Follow the instructions on packaging on how to store food.

Measurements

Imperial measures	Metric measures	Spoon measures
oz = ounce	g = gram	tsp = teaspoon
lb = pound	ml = millilitre	tbsp = tablespoon
fl oz = fluid ounce		

Ask an adult to take hot dishes in and out of the oven.

Healthy eating

You need to eat a balanced diet made up of a variety of different foods, so that you can grow, stay healthy, and have lots of energy for life.

Grains

Bread, cereals, rice, and pasta give you energy. They are grains or made from grains. It's better if you eat the wholegrain types as they contain more minerals and fibre.

Pasta

Pitta bread

Fruits

Your body can get important vitamins and minerals, as well as fibre, from fruits. Fresh, frozen, tinned, or dried – they're all good for you.

Strawberry

Banana

Vegetables

Vegetables are a really important part of a healthy diet. Like fruits, they are full of vitamins, minerals, and fibre. You should eat a variety of vegetables every day.

Broccoli

Carrots

Kidney beans

Meat and beans

We get protein from both animal and plant sources: meat, fish, nuts and seeds, beans, and dairy produce. It's healthy to eat a mixture of these.

Milk products

Dairy items provide valuable vitamins and minerals (such as calcium). Dairy produce includes milk, yoghurt, cheese, butter, cream, and crème fraîche.

Milk

Cheese

Salmon

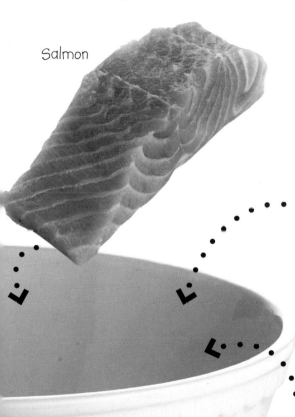

Fats and oils

Everyone needs fat for energy and for their bodies to work properly. The right type of fat is found in olive oil, nuts, seeds, avocados, and oily fish.

Olive oil

Walnuts

Sugary foods and salt

Sugar gives you energy, but eating too much can be bad for you. Too much salt is also linked with health problems.

Biscuits

What is an egg?

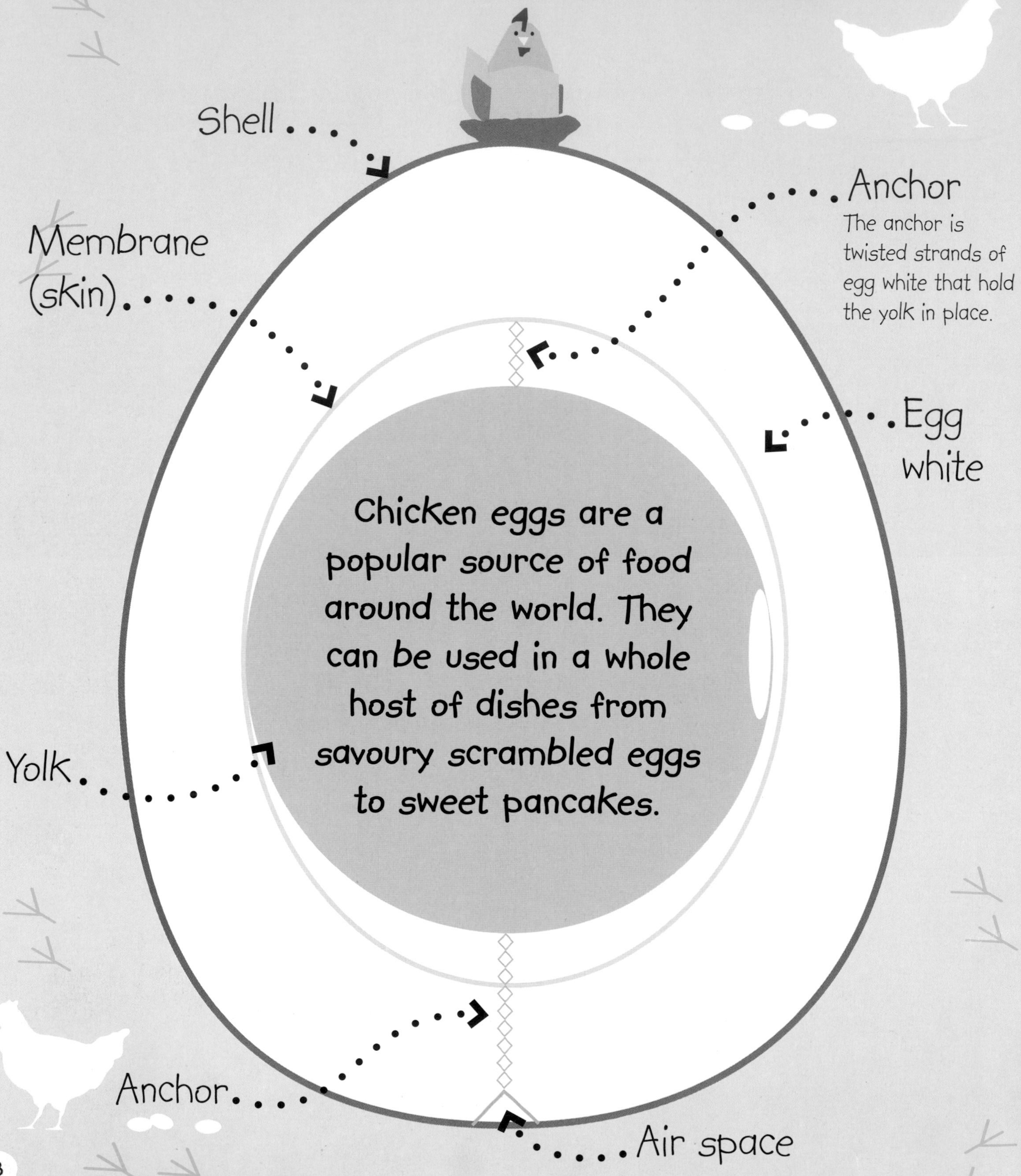

Shell

Membrane (skin)

Anchor

The anchor is twisted strands of egg white that hold the yolk in place.

Egg white

Chicken eggs are a popular source of food around the world. They can be used in a whole host of dishes from savoury scrambled eggs to sweet pancakes.

Yolk

Anchor

Air space

Eggs contain 75 per cent water and 12.5 per cent protein. The rest is made up of vitamins, minerals, fat, and salt.

A chicken can lay up to 259 eggs in one year.

A chicken starts to lay eggs when she's 19 weeks old.

EGGS ARE FULL OF VITAMINS THAT HELP YOUR BODY STAY HEALTHY.

Which do you prefer? The yolk or the white?

Which is your favourite egg to eat?

Chicken egg (brown)   Chicken egg (white)   Duck egg   Quail egg

Eggs and ham

Scrambled eggs are delicious on their own or as part of a cooked breakfast. You can increase the flavour of the dish by adding ham to your scrambled eggs.

You will also need:
- Small knob of butter
- Pinch of salt and freshly ground black pepper

Tools:
- Small bowl
- Fork
- Small frying pan
- Wooden spoon

......1 tbsp milk

1 large egg

.....30g (1oz) chopped ham

Serve with a slice of buttered toast

 You can add fried mushrooms instead of ham.

1 In a small bowl, use a fork to whisk together the egg and milk. Season with salt and pepper.

2 Melt the butter in the pan, over a medium heat. Add the egg mixture. Using the wooden spoon, stir continuously until the eggs are just set and still creamy.

3 Mix in the chopped ham to the eggs. Serve on top of a slice of buttered toast.

5 mins | 12-15 mins | 4 (makes 12)

Pancakes

Pancakes are a splendid treat for breakfast or perfect as a dessert after a light meal. They're incredibly simple and fun to make.

100g (3½oz) self-raising flour

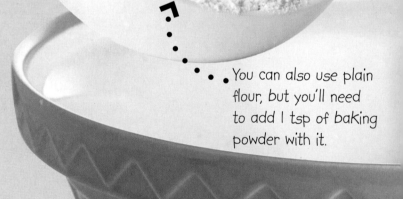

I tsp bicarbonate of soda

Bicarbonate of soda makes the pancakes rise slightly, so that they're fluffy.

You can also use plain flour, but you'll need to add I tsp of baking powder with it.

You will also need:

• Sunflower oil for frying

Tools:

• Sieve
• Large mixing bowl
• Jug
• Fork
• Whisk
• Large non-stick frying pan
• Spatula

150ml (5fl oz) milk

Yummy toppings to try on your pancake

You can use full fat or semi-skimmed milk.

1 egg

Slices of strawberries

Slices of banana

Thinly slice a banana and layer the slices on a pancake before you drizzle syrup on top.

Maple syrup
Blueberries
Icing sugar

1 Sieve the flour and bicarbonate of soda into the bowl and make a well in the centre.

2 Using a fork, lightly beat the egg and milk together in the jug and pour into the well. Whisk the mixture, until you have a smooth batter.

3 Ask an adult to heat one tbsp of oil in a frying pan. Drop large spoonfuls of the batter into the pan.

4 Fry the pancakes for 2 minutes or until golden on the bottom and with bubbles on the top. Flip over to cook the other side.

5 Carefully slice the bananas and strawberries with a table knife. Serve the pancakes with the fruit and maple syrup.

Try out different fruits or serve with slices of bacon instead.

If you don't like syrup
you can use icing sugar.
Sprinkle it lightly over
the pancakes and fruit.

What is flour?

Wheat has been grown for thousands of years. It is ground into a powder which is called flour. Flour is the key ingredient for making bread, pastries, cakes, biscuits, and pasta. The main types of flour are; self-raising, plain, brown or wholemeal, and strong bread flour.

Spikelet ......

Beard ......

Stem ......

...... Leaf

Wheat is grown in large fields. It is a strong type of grass. Each plant yields between 20-50 kernels of grain.

This diagram shows a close-up of the head (or spike) of a wheat plant. Wheat spikes are made up of a number of spikelets, that bear one to five flowers. The flowers turn into kernels.

Modern farmers use combine harvesters to harvest (collect) their wheat.

The grain exits the harvester from the chute at the back, usually into a wagon.

The blades in the cutter bar cut down the wheat. It goes up into the machine on a conveyor belt.

The grain is separated from the chaff and straw by a thresher.

Once harvested, grain is taken to a factory where it is ground into flour. The flour is then packaged and sold in shops.

To make it last longer, flour should be stored in a cool, dry, dark place.

17

Star cookies

40 mins (including 10 mins chilling) 10-12 mins 16 (depending on cookie cutters)

These ginger and orange star cookies have a real zing to them. You'll have lots of fun cutting them out of the dough and decorating them with coloured icing.

125g (4oz) butter, cubed

100g (3½oz) caster sugar

Small cubes of butter are easier to rub into flour than a big block.

2 tbsp golden syrup

18

1 tsp ground ginger....

You can use a teaspoon of ground cinnamon if you don't like ginger.

250g (9oz) plain flour, sieved

Finely grated zest of 1 orange....

....1 medium egg, lightly beaten

Follow the steps on the next page to see which ingredients you put into the bowl first.

Tools:

- 2 large baking sheets
- Baking parchment
- Large mixing bowl
- Wooden spoon
- Rolling pin
- Star shape cutters
- Cooling rack
- Small bowl

To decorate:

- 300g (10oz) royal icing sugar
- 2-3 tbsp water
- 2-3 drops food colouring

1 Ask an adult to preheat the oven to 180°C (350°F/ Gas 4). Line 2 baking sheets with parchment. In a bowl, rub the flour and butter together until they resemble breadcrumbs.

2 Mix in the *sugar*, *ginger*, and *orange rind*. In a small bowl, beat the *egg* and *golden syrup* with a fork, then add to the mixture. Stir with a wooden spoon until it forms a ball.

3 Wrap in cling film and chill in the fridge for 10 minutes. Roll out the dough on a lightly floured surface to 4–5mm (1/4in) thickness. Cut into stars using cookie cutters (*see pages 22–23*).

4 Place the stars slightly apart on the baking trays and *bake for 10–12 minutes* until golden. Allow to cool on the trays for 2 minutes, then transfer to a cooling rack.

5 Sift the *icing sugar* into a mixing bowl and slowly stir in enough *water* to create a smooth mixture. Divide into 3 bowls. Stir in the *colourings* to make 3 different icings.

6 Carefully spread the icing onto the biscuits using a knife or drizzle over using a teaspoon or piping bag to create stripes and patterns. Set aside until the icing sets.

If you prefer, try lemon rind instead of orange.

You can place cutters right up to the edge of the dough.

Reroll the extra trimmings to make more stars.

Dust the cookie cutters with flour.

To avoid sticking, dust your rolling pin with flour.

Blueberry sponge

Sponge cakes are ideal for birthdays or other special occasions. They can be filled with a fruit of your choice. We've chosen juicy blueberries.

100ml (3½fl oz) double cream

4 tbsp blueberry jam or conserve

175g (6oz) blueberries

Reserve a handful, to decorate the top of the cake.

Icing sugar, to dust.

225g (8oz)
caster sugar

 20 mins | 25 mins | 8-10

Tools:
- 2 x 20cm (8in) round sandwich tins
- Scissors and baking parchment
- Large mixing bowl
- Electric hand whisk
- Sieve
- Large metal spoon
- Wire cooling rack
- Medium mixing bowl
- Hand whisk

Use butter at room temperature, instead of straight from the fridge, because it will be easier to beat into the mixture.

225g (8oz)
softened butter

225g (8oz)
self-raising
flour

4 large eggs,
lightly beaten

25

1 Ask an adult to preheat the oven to 180°C (350°F/ Gas 4). Draw around the tin twice on the parchment and cut out. Grease the parchment and line both tins.

2 Place the butter and sugar in a large mixing bowl and beat with the electric whisk until light and creamy.

3 Add a little of the eggs and whisk in. Repeat until the egg mixture has all been added.

4 Sift the flour into the mixture. Use a metal spoon to fold it together until all the flour has disappeared.

5 Divide the mixture between the tins, levelling the tops with the back of the spoon. Bake for 25 minutes, or until risen and firm to the touch.

6 Leave to cool briefly in the tins then turn out onto a wire rack to cool. Remove the baking parchment and allow the cake to cool completely.

For an alternative filling, you can use sliced strawberries instead of blueberries.

Serve the cake in slices of equal size.

Finishing touches

Whisk the cream in a bowl, with the hand whisk, until it forms soft peaks. Spread the flat side of one cake with jam, then top with cream and blueberries. Place the other cake on top. To decorate, add a handful of blueberries and sift icing sugar over the cake.

Cheesy bread rolls

These bread rolls are simple and fun to make. The melted cheese on top of each roll adds a lot of flavour to the bread. You can eat the rolls plain, or fill them with sandwich fillings.

250g (9oz) strong white bread flour

350ml (12fl oz) tepid water......

........2 tsp dried active yeast

2 hours 20 mins | 25–30 mins | 9

1 tsp caster sugar...

250g (9oz) strong wholemeal bread flour

Wholemeal bread flour has tiny bits of grain in it. This gives the bread a more interesting texture...

Ingredients to serve:

- 9 lettuce leaves
- 2 tomatoes, sliced
- 5 slices of ham
- 4 slices of Cheddar cheese

Tools:

- Small bowl
- Teaspoon
- Large mixing bowl
- Wooden spoon
- Clean tea towel
- Large baking sheet
- Pastry brush

...1½ tsp salt

Items to top your rolls with before baking

75g (2½oz) grated mature Cheddar cheese...

1 egg, beaten

29

1 Pour 100ml (3½fl oz) of the water into a small bowl. Sprinkle in the yeast and sugar and stir until dissolved. Leave in a warm place for 5 minutes or until *bubbles* appear on the surface.

2 Put both types of flour and the salt into a large bowl and use a spoon to mix together. Use your hand to make a well in the centre.

3 Pour the yeast and most of the remaining water into the well and gently mix together to form a soft dough. Stir in the extra water if it is too dry.

4 Turn the dough out onto a floured surface. Knead firmly using the heel of your hand, folding the dough over as you go. Knead for 10 minutes until smooth and shiny. Put the dough in a clean bowl and cover with a tea towel. Leave to rise in a warm place, for 1½–2 hours until doubled in size.

5 Ask an adult to preheat the oven to 220°C (425°F/Gas 7). Knock back the risen dough with your knuckles, by punching down on it.

6 Divide the dough into 9 equal pieces. Dust your hands with a little flour and shape the dough into rolls.

7 Place the rolls on a greased baking sheet, cover with a damp tea towel and leave for 10 minutes.

8 Brush the rolls with the egg and press the cheese on top of each roll. Bake for 25–30 minutes, or until risen and golden.

 Allow to cool slightly before filling with whatever you fancy.

What is pasta?

Pasta is made by mixing finely sieved flour, olive oil, and egg. Pasta is produced in factories, but can also be made at home using a pasta machine or by cutting it by hand to make different types. Pasta is yummy and fills you up!

Olive oil **+** Flour **+** Egg

=

Flour, olive oil, and egg are mixed together to form a dough.

Dough

The dough is rolled out and passed through the machine. As the handle gets turned the dough is squeezed by the rollers. Different cutting attachments are used to make a variety of pasta types.

Pasta machine

Which is your favourite type of pasta?

Conchiglie rigate
(shell)

Farfalle
(butterfly shape)

Fusilli (twists)

Wholewheat
penne

Rigatoni (large
grooved macaroni)

Macaroni
(narrow tubes)

Penne rigate
(striped quill)

Stelline
(little stars)

Ruote tricolore
(wheels)

Tortiglione
(hollow spiral)

Tortelloni (usually stuffed
with cheese or vegetables)

Pansotti (pot-bellied
dumplings)

Spinach trottole
(trottole means "spins")

Cappellacci (stuffed
with a pumpkin filling)

Tortelli anolini
(half-moon-shaped bundle)

Vermicelli nest

Cannelloni (stuffed
with sauce and meat)

Tagliatelle (thin and
delicate flat noodles)

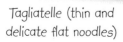

Spaghetti (thin string)

Lasagne sheets

Cooking pasta

Pasta forms the base of many popular dishes, so it's important you know the right way to cook it. If you don't cook it long enough it has a crunch and if you over-cook it then it becomes soggy!

1 Ask an adult to bring slightly salted water to the boil in a large saucepan.

2 Choose the type of pasta you want for your meal and ask an adult to add the correct quantity to the boiling water. Cook the pasta for 10–12 minutes (or less time if the packaging states it).

 Smaller pasta shapes will take less time to cook.

3 Ask an adult to use a slotted spoon to take out a piece for you to test that it's ready. It should be soft, but not soggy. Let it cool before you try it. Ask an adult to pour the pasta into a colander to be drained.

Use fresh, warm running water to rinse the pasta.

15 mins | 20 mins | 4-6

Pasta bake

This pasta bake is perfect for a healthy family meal. Serve it with a crisp green salad to add a bit of veg. The meatballs are super-easy and fun to make and it will instantly become a family favourite.

2 tbsp chopped fresh parsley

2 tbsp freshly grated Parmesan cheese

350g (12oz) lean minced beef

You can also make your own breadcrumbs by toasting a slice of bread and whizzing it up in a food processor.

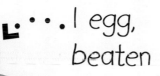

1 tbsp dried breadcrumbs

You will also need:

• Salt and freshly ground pepper
• 1 tbsp olive oil
• 1 quantity tomato pasta sauce (see pages 52–53)

To serve:

• Crisp green salad

Tools:

• Large mixing bowl
• Wooden spoon
• Medium saucepan
• Large saucepan
• Large ovenproof dish

125g (4½oz) ball mozzarella, drained and roughly chopped

1 egg, beaten

250g (9oz) dried rigatoni or penne pasta

1 Place the beef, egg, parsley, Parmesan, and breadcrumbs in the bowl. Season with salt and pepper. Use your hands to combine the mixture.

2 Use your hands to roll the mixture into 24 small balls. Set aside.

3 Ask an adult to cook the pasta in a saucepan of slightly salted boiling water for 10–12 minutes until tender. Drain well.

4 Ask an adult to heat the oil in the large pan and lightly brown the meatballs, in 2 batches. Return the meatballs to the pan. Add the sauce, cover, and simmer for 5 minutes.

5 Carefully stir the pasta into the meatball mixture, then transfer to the ovenproof dish.

6 Tear the cheese and sprinkle over the top of the dish. Ask an adult to cook it under a preheated hot grill for 3–4 minutes, until the cheese has melted. Serve with a salad.

You can also use turkey or pork mince instead of beef to make the meatballs.

What is rice?

Rice is the staple (main) food for almost half the people in the world. It has a mild flavour so it goes with lots of food. It keeps for a long time and when it's cooked it can be sticky or fluffy.

Rice grows in paddy fields that are flooded with water. The water helps to stop weeds from growing in the fields.

Rice has two outer layers. The hull is on the outside, underneath is the bran, followed by the white rice.

White rice

Hull

Bran

Germ

Rice takes about 4 months to grow. It's picked by hand or combine harvester.

White rice has had the bran removed. Brown rice still has its layer of bran.

SHORTGRAIN RICE IS EASY TO EAT WITH CHOPSTICKS BECAUSE THE GRAINS ARE SOFT AND STICK TOGETHER.

Which is your favourite type of rice?

Long grain rice is light and fluffy when cooked.

Basmati rice is used a lot in Indian style cooking.

Paella rice, as its name suggests, is used to make paellas.

Carnaroli rice is often used to make risottos.

Short grain rice is creamy when cooked and is used for rice puddings.

Despite its name, wild rice isn't actually rice!

Chicken risotto

10 mins · 20 mins · 4

Risotto dishes use hot stock to soak through and cook the rice, meat, and vegetables. This makes the meal incredibly tasty!

75g (2½oz) reduced-fat soft cream cheese

2 tbsp chopped parsley

1 small onion, chopped

2 tbsp freshly grated Parmesan cheese

900ml (1½ pints) hot chicken or vegetable stock

44

225g (7½oz) basmati rice.......

Risottos are usually made with arborio rice, but we have used basmati.

Chicken risotto

3 boneless, skinless chicken breasts, cubed

75g (2½oz) frozen peas.......

100g (3½oz) tinned sweetcorn, drained

You will also need:
• Small knob of butter
• 1 tbsp sunflower oil

Tools:
• Sieve • Small sharp knife
• Medium saucepan with lid
• Chopping board • Wooden spoon

45

1 Place the rice in a sieve. Rinse the rice under running cold water, until the water runs clear. Drain well.

2 Heat the butter and oil in the saucepan, add the onion and cook for 2–3 minutes. Stir in the chicken and cook until lightly browned.

3 Add the rice to the pan, stir to coat in the oil, and cook for 1 minute, until the rice is transparent.

4 Add half of the stock and cook, over a low heat, until most of the liquid has been absorbed, stirring occasionally.

5 Stir in the remaining stock and cook until the stock has been absorbed and the rice is tender, this should take 10–12 minutes. Stir in the peas and corn and cook for 2–3 minutes.

6 Stir in the cream cheese, parsley, and Parmesan. Season to taste and serve immediately in bowls.

Leave out the chicken for a veggie version. Add more vegetables, meat-free sausages, or tofu.

What is a tomato?

A tomato is the fruit of a tomato plant, but in cooking it's always called a vegetable. Tomatoes are used in many ways: as the base for sauces and soups, or as part of a salad. Tomatoes come in several shapes, colours, and sizes.

Flower

Node

Leaf

Fruit

Shoot

Root

Primary root

Lateral root

The roots of a tomato plant grow underground and the shoot grows above. Tomato plants need lots of sunshine and water to thrive.

25 tomatoes are used to make one bottle of tomato sauce.

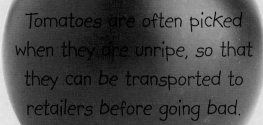

Tomatoes are often picked when they are unripe, so that they can be transported to retailers before going bad.

The tomato was first eaten in South America, before it became popular globally.

IN ELIZABETHAN TIMES, TOMATOES WERE THOUGHT TO BE BAD FOR YOU. NOW WE THINK THE OPPOSITE.

Vine ripened tomato

Beef tomato

Cherry tomatoes

Yellow tomato

Green zebra tomato

Baby plum tomato

Tomberries

Preparing tomatoes

In order to make certain recipes you need to know how to get the ingredients ready. Tomatoes can be used in many ways, so it's important to learn how to prepare them properly.

How to slice a tomato

Use a sharp knife to cut the first slice off one end of the tomato. Cut the rest of the tomato into slices of similar thickness.

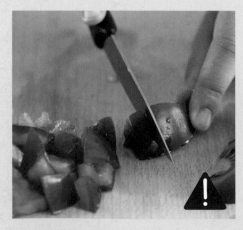

How to cube a tomato

Cut a tomato in half vertically. Slice the halves into wedges of equal size. Then cut each individual wedge into cubes.

How to skin a tomato

Tomatoes will not ripen in the fridge, so keep them at room temperature for the best colour and flavour.

★ 1 Cut a cross on the top of a tomato. Place the tomato in a bowl. Cover with boiled water and leave for 10 seconds.

★ 2 Drain the water from the bowl and place the tomato into a bowl of cold water. When the tomato is cool enough to handle, peel off the skin.

Tomatoes are usually red, but some varieties are yellow or purple.

Tomatoes are amazingly versatile. How will you use yours?

How to deseed a tomato

Cut a tomato in half horizontally. Use your fingers to scoop out the seeds and juice over a small bowl.

Tomato sauce

10 mins | 20 mins | 4

Most pasta dishes have a tomato-based sauce. Meat or vegetables are often added to the sauce to add variety, but pasta and tomato sauce are also perfect on their own.

You will also need:
- Salt and freshly ground black pepper
- 1 tsp sugar

Tools:
- Medium saucepan
- Wooden spoon

2 x 400g (14oz) cans chopped tomatoes

1 clove garlic, crushed

2 tbsp tomato purée

1 onion, chopped

Small handful of fresh basil

2 tbsp olive oil

1 Ask an adult to heat the oil in the saucepan, over a medium heat. Add the onion and garlic and cook for 4–5 minutes until softened, but not browned.

2 Stir in the tomatoes, tomato purée, and sugar. Bring to the boil, then reduce the heat and simmer, uncovered, for 15 minutes, stirring occasionally.

3 Using your hands, tear the basil leaves into small pieces. Stir into the sauce and season to taste.

53

Pitta pizzas

Pizza sauce is easy to make. Spread one tablespoon of it on a pitta bread (that's been grilled for a minute). Add grated mozzarella and any other toppings you fancy. Ask an adult to grill it for five minutes.

To make the pizza sauce, you will need:

- 200ml (7fl oz) passata
- 2 tbsp tomato purée
- ½ tsp sugar
- 1 tsp dried mixed herbs
- Small saucepan
- Wooden spoon

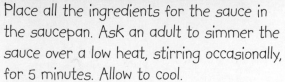

Place all the ingredients for the sauce in the saucepan. Ask an adult to simmer the sauce over a low heat, stirring occasionally, for 5 minutes. Allow to cool.

For the toppings:

- 4 tbsp pizza sauce (1 tbsp per pitta)
- 4 handfuls of grated mozzarella
- 1 slice of ham, cut into strips
- 1 handful of sweetcorn
- 1 slice of pineapple, cut into chunks
- 5 pieces of pepperoni
- 1 slice of green, red, and yellow pepper, diced
- 4 cherry tomatoes, sliced
- 3 fresh basil leaves, to garnish
- 1 handful of chargrilled chicken pieces
- 1 mushroom, sliced and fried
- 4 strips of red pepper

Which pizza toppings will you choose?

Ham, sweetcorn, and pineapple

Pepperoni and peppers

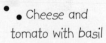

Cheese and tomato with basil

Chicken, mushroom, and red pepper

Lay out your ingredients, ready to make your pizzas.

What is a potato?

A potato is a vegetable that grows underneath the ground. Potatoes come in a variety of types and sizes. They are a popular food around the world and are prepared to eat in a range of ways.

Flower

Leaflets

Stem

Roots

Underground stem

Developing tuber

2-6 weeks after planting, shoots begin to push out of the soil. Under the ground, potatoes (called tubers) form.

Fully expanded tuber

Roots

Old seed place

Potatoes can be diced, sliced, cubed, and grated. They can be fried, boiled, mashed, steamed, or roasted!

The flower of a potato plant is toxic. Certain types of potato plants produce small green fruits. Don't eat them though as they are poisonous!

The layer just inside the skin is the most nutritious part, so always use a potato peeler to avoid cutting too deep and losing all the nutrients.

POTATOES ARE SO POPULAR IN BRITAIN, THAT PEOPLE GET ALMOST A QUARTER OF THEIR VITAMIN C INTAKE FROM THEM.

Potatoes are only loosely related to sweet potatoes, because the latter is a root vegetable.

King Edward......

Maris Piper......

Sweet potatoes

Miniature potatoes......

Baby Jersey

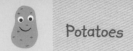

Potato fishcakes

Creamy mashed potatoes and salmon covered in crispy breadcrumbs make this dish delicious.

1 tbsp fresh parsley, chopped ....⌐

250g (9oz) potatoes, peeled .....⌐

Cut the potatoes into 5cm (2in) pieces.

2 spring onions, trimmed and finely chopped .....⌐

2 tsp Dijon mustard

85g (3oz) plain flour

60-70 mins

40 mins

4

150g (5½oz) dried breadcrumbs

You will also need:

- Freshly ground black pepper
- Pinch of salt
- 6 tbsp sunflower oil
- Salad, to serve
- Lemon wedges, to serve

Tools:

- Medium saucepan
- Colander
- Masher
- Mixing bowl
- Fork
- Wooden spoon
- Large plate
- Cling film
- Dish
- 2 medium plates
- Large frying pan
- Fish slice
- Kitchen paper

350g (12oz) tinned pink salmon, drained weight

2 eggs

1 Half fill the saucepan with water. Add the potatoes and a pinch of salt. Ask an adult to bring it to the boil and cook for 12-15 minutes.

2 Drain the potatoes in the colander and put them back in the pan. Mash until smooth and leave them until they are cool enough to handle.

3 Break the salmon into small pieces in a bowl, removing the skin and bones. Stir in the potatoes, mustard, spring onions, and parsley. Season.

4 Lightly dust your hands with a little flour and shape the mixture into 8 cakes. Place on a plate, cover with cling film and chill in the fridge for 30 minutes.

5 Beat the eggs. Put the flour and breadcrumbs on separate plates. Coat each fishcake in flour, then egg, and then the breadcrumbs. Ask an adult to preheat the oven to a low heat.

6 Ask an adult to heat half the oil in a large pan on a medium heat. Shallow fry 4 of the cakes for 2-3 minutes on each side or until golden. Keep them warm in the oven. Repeat with the other cakes.

Serve the fishcakes with a wedge of lemon and a mixed-leaf salad.

What is a pea?

Peas are a popular vegetable to grow and eat. There are two main types to try. The garden pea is shelled from its pod before being eaten, but podded peas, such as mangetout or sugar snap peas, are eaten with the pod intact.

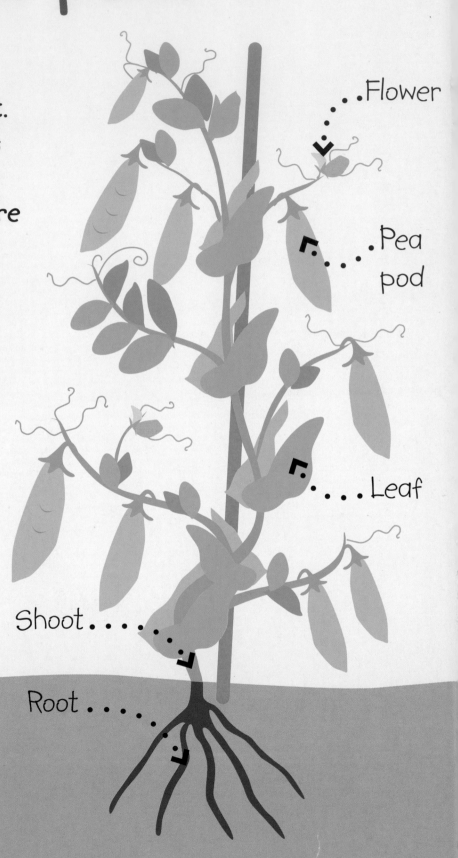

Flower

Pea pod

Leaf

Shoot......

Root......

Peas grow on vine-like plants. When the flower drops off, a pea pod grows in its place. The peas grow inside the pod until they're ready to pick.

Shelling peas

Press down gently on one end of the pod to open it up.

Use your thumb to push down one side of the pod to reveal the peas.

Use your thumb to push down inside the pod, so that all the peas come out.

Peas are green because they are picked before they are ripe. A ripe pea is more yellow than green in colour.

Once picked, peas can be kept in the refrigerator or freezer. Only 5 per cent of peas picked are sold fresh. Most are frozen or tinned.

Sugar snap peas...

Garden pea pods...

Mangetout peas...

Garden peas

5 mins · 3 mins · 6

Pea houmous

This pea houmous is incredibly tasty and full of flavour. Packed with protein and vitamins, this dip is perfect for a healthy snack or as a side dish to accompany lunch or dinner.

You will also need:
- Salt and freshly ground black pepper
- Vegetables, to serve

Tools:
- Medium saucepan
- Sieve
- Food processor
- Bowl or 3 paper cups

1 tbsp tahini

Juice of 1 lemon

2 tbsp olive oil

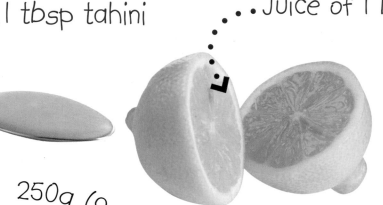

250g (9oz) frozen peas

400g (14oz) can chickpeas, drained

64

1 Cook the peas in a saucepan of boiling water, for 3 minutes. Carefully drain through a sieve, then refresh under cold water.

2 Place all the ingredients in a food processor and blend until smooth and creamy. Season with salt and pepper. Use a teaspoon to test a small amount. Transfer to a bowl or into two paper cups to serve.

Serve with sliced vegetables such as carrots, peppers, celery, and mangetout.

What is chocolate?

Chocolate is made from cocoa beans, the seeds of the cacao tree that grow in tropical forests. Cocoa beans were first used to make a bitter drink, which is the opposite to the sweet hot chocolate we drink today and the creamy bars we love to eat!

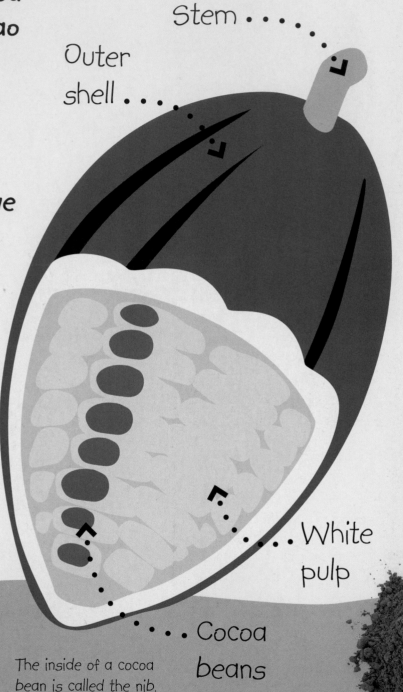

Stem

Outer shell

White pulp

Cocoa beans

The inside of a cocoa bean is called the nib.

Cocoa pods grow on the main branches and trunk of the cacao tree. They grow to the size of a melon and take 4–5 months to ripen.

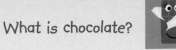

HOW IS MILK CHOCOLATE MADE?

Start with cocoa mass,

then add sugar

followed by full-fat milk,

add cocoa butter.

Mix everything together

and you get chocolate!

Milk chocolate is the same as dark chocolate, but with milk added.

White chocolate contains cocoa butter, not cocoa mass (ground cocoa beans), so isn't always thought to be true chocolate.

Cocoa powder is made from ground cocoa beans that have had the cocoa butter removed.

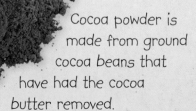

Dark chocolate is cocoa mass mixed with sugar and cocoa butter.

Chocolate truffles

Create these amazing truffles as Christmas presents for friends and family. Make 6 gift boxes and put 4 truffles in each box. Everyone will be impressed with how delicious and pretty your truffles are.

15g (½oz) unsalted butter

Make sure you use double cream, single cream is too runny and won't work.

150ml (5½fl oz) double cream

5 mins | 125 mins | Makes 24 truffles

You'll need icing sugar to dust your hands with.

 You can also make these truffles using milk or dark chocolate.

 **300g (10oz) white chocolate (30% cocoa)**

To decorate:

Choose from
- Sifted cocoa powder
- Grated milk, plain, and white chocolate
- Chocolate pieces
- Sugar sprinkles
- Chopped nuts e.g. pistachios, toasted hazelnuts
- Desiccated coconut

Tools:

- Baking sheet
- Baking parchment
- Medium sized bowl
- Small saucepan
- Wooden spoon
- Teaspoon
- Sieve

Make sure you use a big enough bowl to fit all the ingredients in.

1 Line the baking sheet with baking parchment. Break the chocolate into small pieces in the bowl and set aside. Put the cream in the small saucepan with the butter and ask an adult to bring it slowly to the boil. Then pour the cream over the broken chocolate.

2 With a wooden spoon, stir until the mixture is smooth and all the chocolate has melted. Cover and allow the mixture to cool for about 10 minutes at room temperature. Then transfer to a fridge to chill for about 2 hours, until firm enough to handle.

 Be creative and come up with other toppings to roll your truffles in.

3 Using a teaspoon, scoop out bite-sized pieces of the chocolate mixture.

4 Dust your hands lightly with icing sugar so that they don't stick to the chocolate. Roll into balls and place on the baking sheet.

5 Roll the truffles in sifted cocoa powder or grated chocolate, sprinkles, nuts, or coconut. Place in individual sweet cases and chill. They will keep for up to 10 days in an airtight container. Store them in the fridge as they contain cream.

What's your favourite truffle?

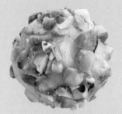

Rolled in chopped pistachio nuts

Dusted with cocoa powder

Sprinkled with desiccated coconut

Rolled in dark chocolate pieces

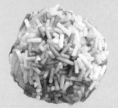

Covered in colourful sprinkles

Rolled in grated chocolate

These chocolate truffles are so delicious, they will melt in your mouth.

20 mins | 2-3 mins | 4

Chocolate dip

Fruit dipped in chocolate is a sweet treat that everyone will like. Make this dish for a party. Everyone can get dipping and share in the chocolatey fun!

You will also need:
- ½ cantaloupe melon, seeds scooped out (use a melon baller to make balls from the fruit)
- 1 pineapple, sliced into chunks
- 2 mangoes, cubed
- 3 kiwi fruit, sliced

Tools:
- Small saucepan
- Small grater
- Wooden spoon
- Serving bowl
- 2 large plates
- Wooden skewers

125g (4½oz) good quality milk chocolate

The chocolate should be 32 per cent cocoa. Break it into small pieces.

150ml (5fl oz) double cream

2 tbsp golden syrup

1 lime

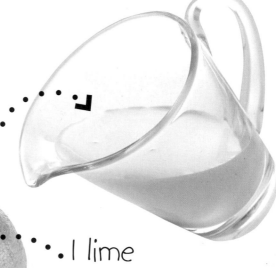

1 Place the chocolate, cream, and golden syrup in the pan and finely grate over the rind of the lime.

2 Cook on a low heat, stirring until all the chocolate has melted and you have a smooth sauce. Pour into a serving bowl and allow to cool.

Arrange the fruit onto 2 large plates. Using skewers, dip the fruit in the chocolate dip.

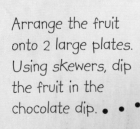

What is a strawberry?

Strawberries are a popular fruit to grow and eat around the world. The sweet flavour, soft texture, and juice content of a strawberry makes it perfect for use in drinks, desserts, jams, and sauces.

Flower.

The strawberry fruit grows as the petals fall away.

Fruit

Leaf.

Strawberries need moist conditions to grow in. They should be planted in dappled shade or in direct sunlight in order to thrive.

Stem.

Runner

Roots.

The garden strawberry that we eat today was first cultivated in France in the 1750s.

A SERVING OF EIGHT STRAWBERRIES CONTAINS MORE VITAMIN C THAN ONE ORANGE.

Strawberries are a traditional dessert served in Sweden on Midsummer Eve.

Strawberries are the only fruit that have seeds on the outside.

In Roman times, strawberries were used as a medicine.

28,000kg (987,671oz) strawberries are eaten at the annual tennis tournament in Wimbledon, UK.

Smoothie time

5 mins   4

Smoothies are a yummy snack or a breakfast drink. They are easy and quick to make and you can experiment with your own choices of ingredients.

Tools:
- Table knife
- Chopping board
- Blender

250g (9oz) fat free vanilla yoghurt

1 ripe banana

200ml (7fl oz) semi-skimmed milk

It's important that you rinse strawberries before you eat them.

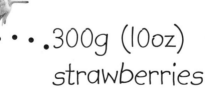

300g (10oz) strawberries

Hull the strawberries first, by taking out the stems.

⭐1 Use a table knife to cut the strawberries in half and set aside. Peel the banana and roughly chop into chunks.

⭐2 Carefully place the strawberries and banana in a blender with the vanilla yoghurt and the milk. Put the lid on securely. Whizz until the mixture is thick and smooth, then pour into glasses. Serve at once.

Freeze your smoothies for a cool treat!

Once you've made your smoothie mixture you can pour it into 4 moulds to make the most delicious ice lollies, ready for a hot day.

It's best to drink a smoothie straight after it's made. If you let it sit for too long, you'll need to stir it to remix the ingredients.

Index

Acknowledgements

With thanks to: Jennifer Lane for additional editing, Tamsin Weston for additional prop styling, Katie Federico for assisting at a photo shoot, and Jo Casey for proofreading.

Photos courtesy of: Peter Anderson, Philip Dowell, Will Heap, Ian O'Leary, Richard Leeney, Gary Ombler, William Shaw, and Linda Whitwam. All other images © Dorling Kindersley

With special thanks to the models: Roberto Barney Allen, Abi and Kate Arnold, Lara Duffy, James and Ying Glover, Kathryn Meeker, Ella and Eva Menzie and Oliver Tran.